This Notebook Belongs To:

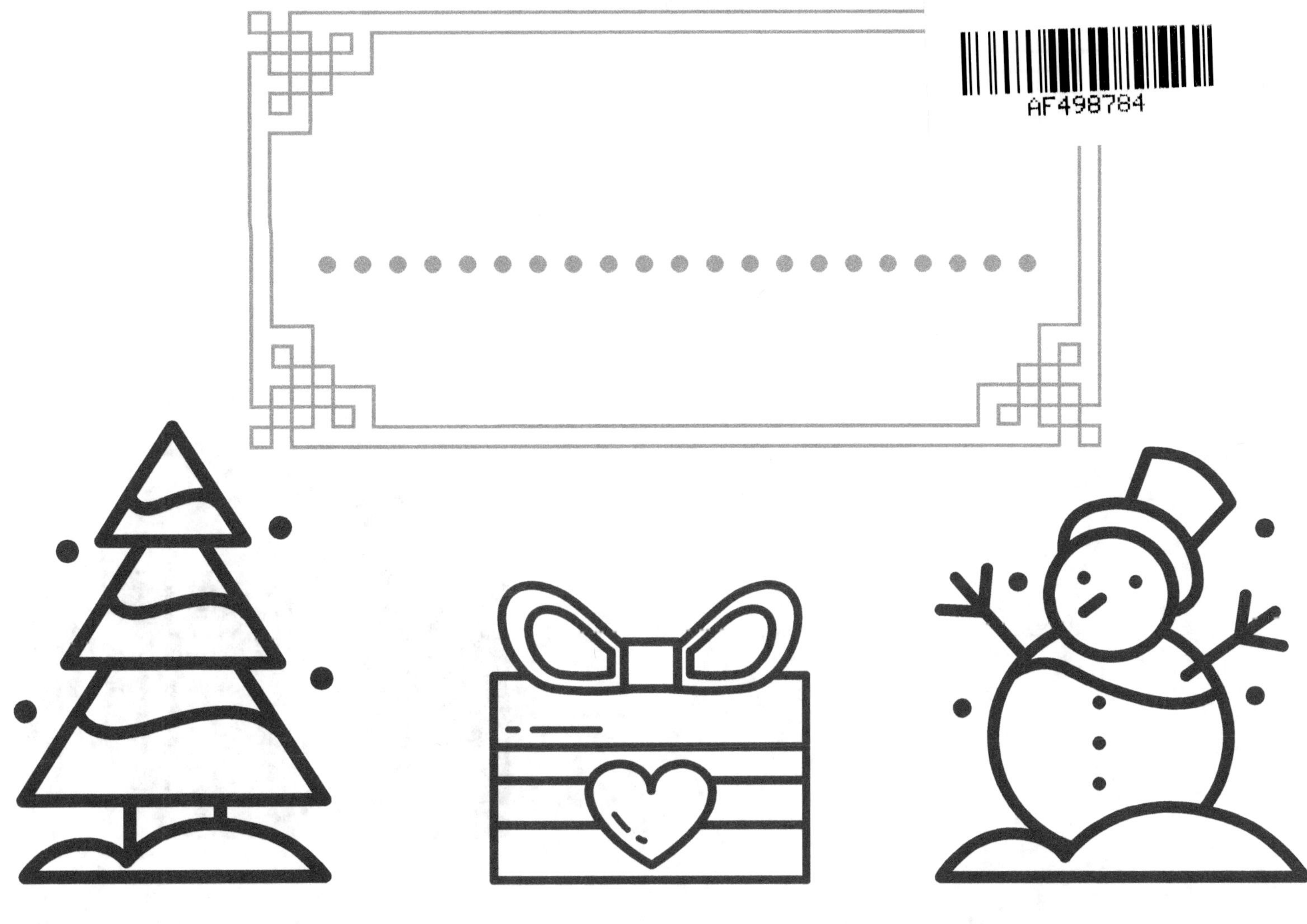

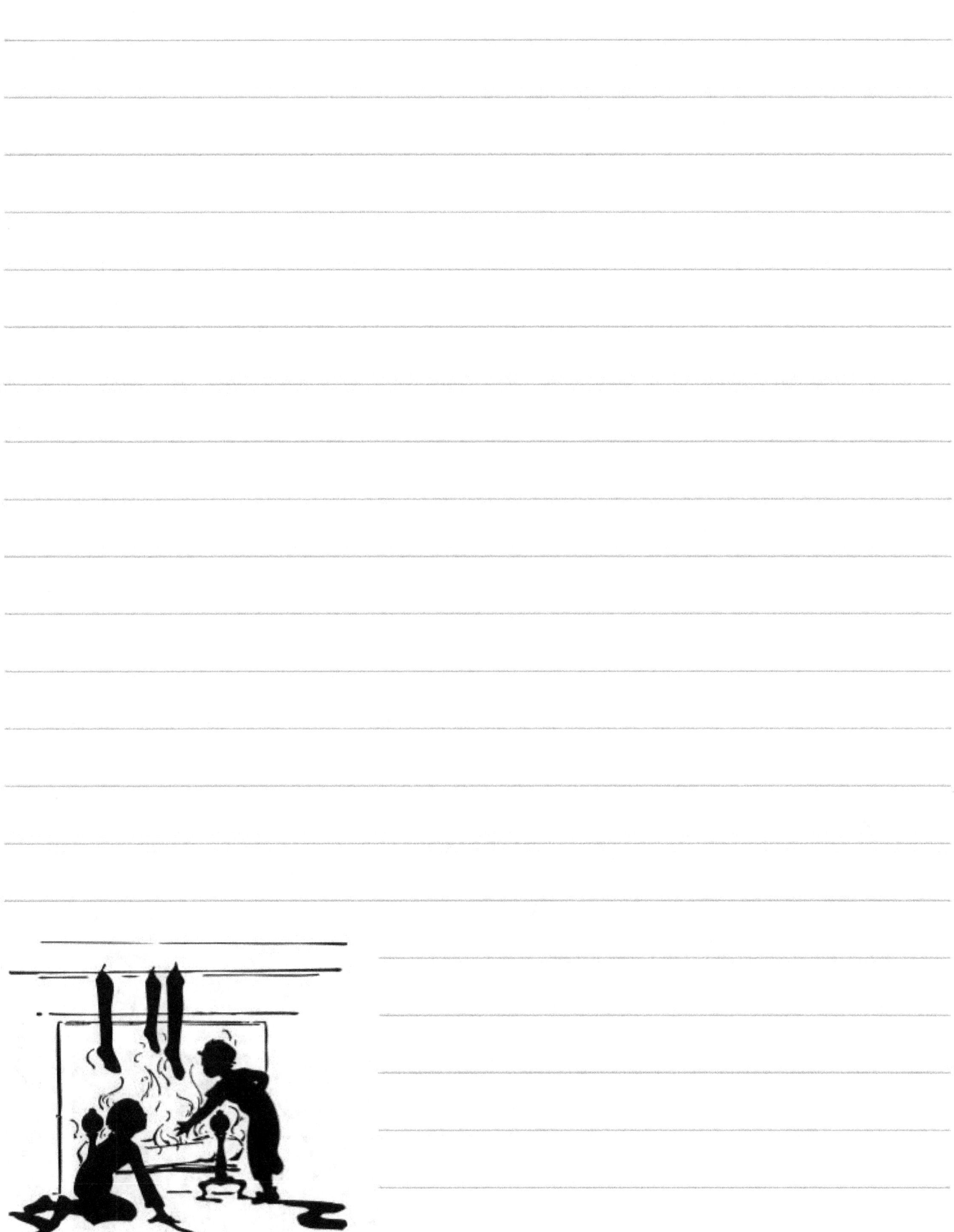

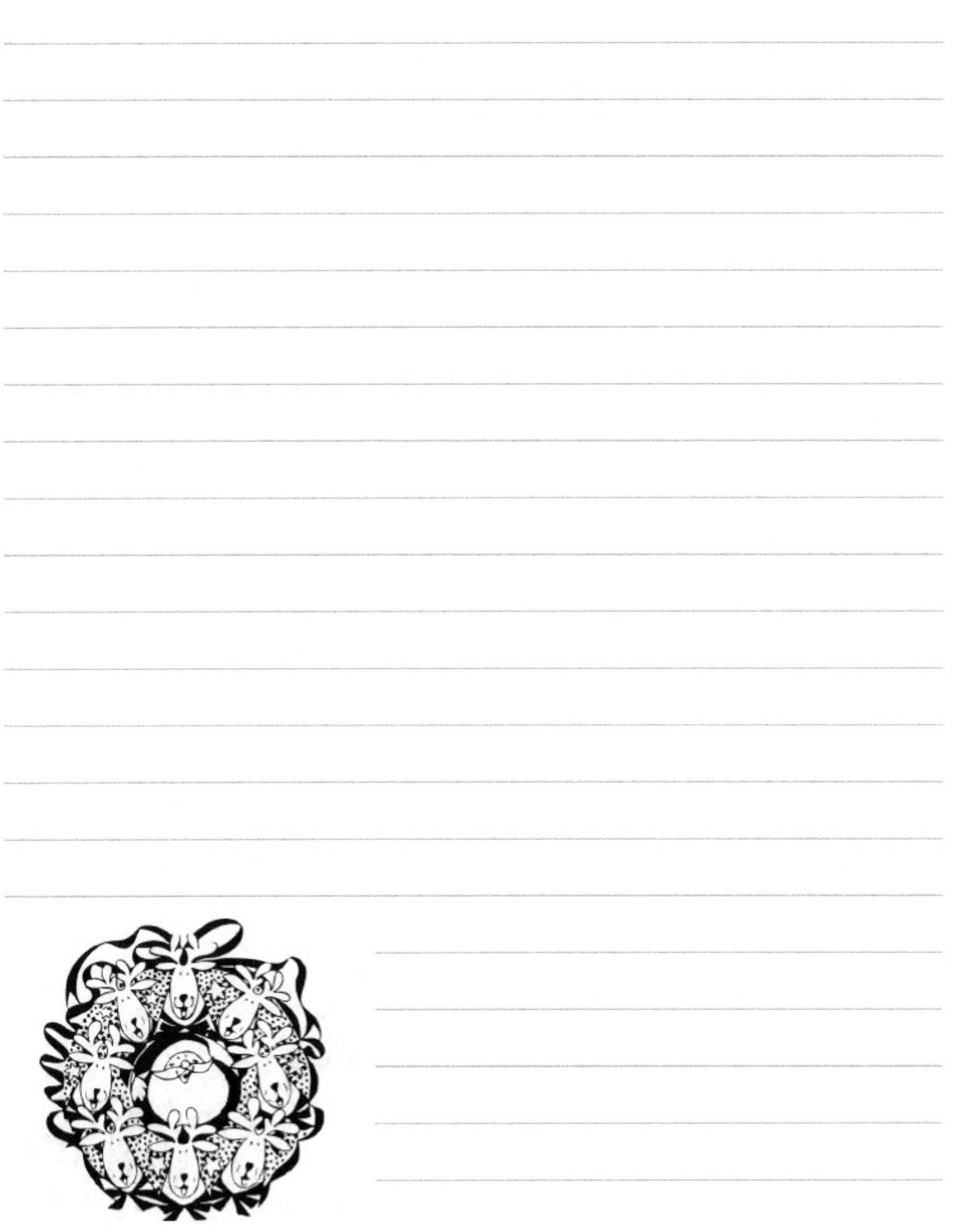

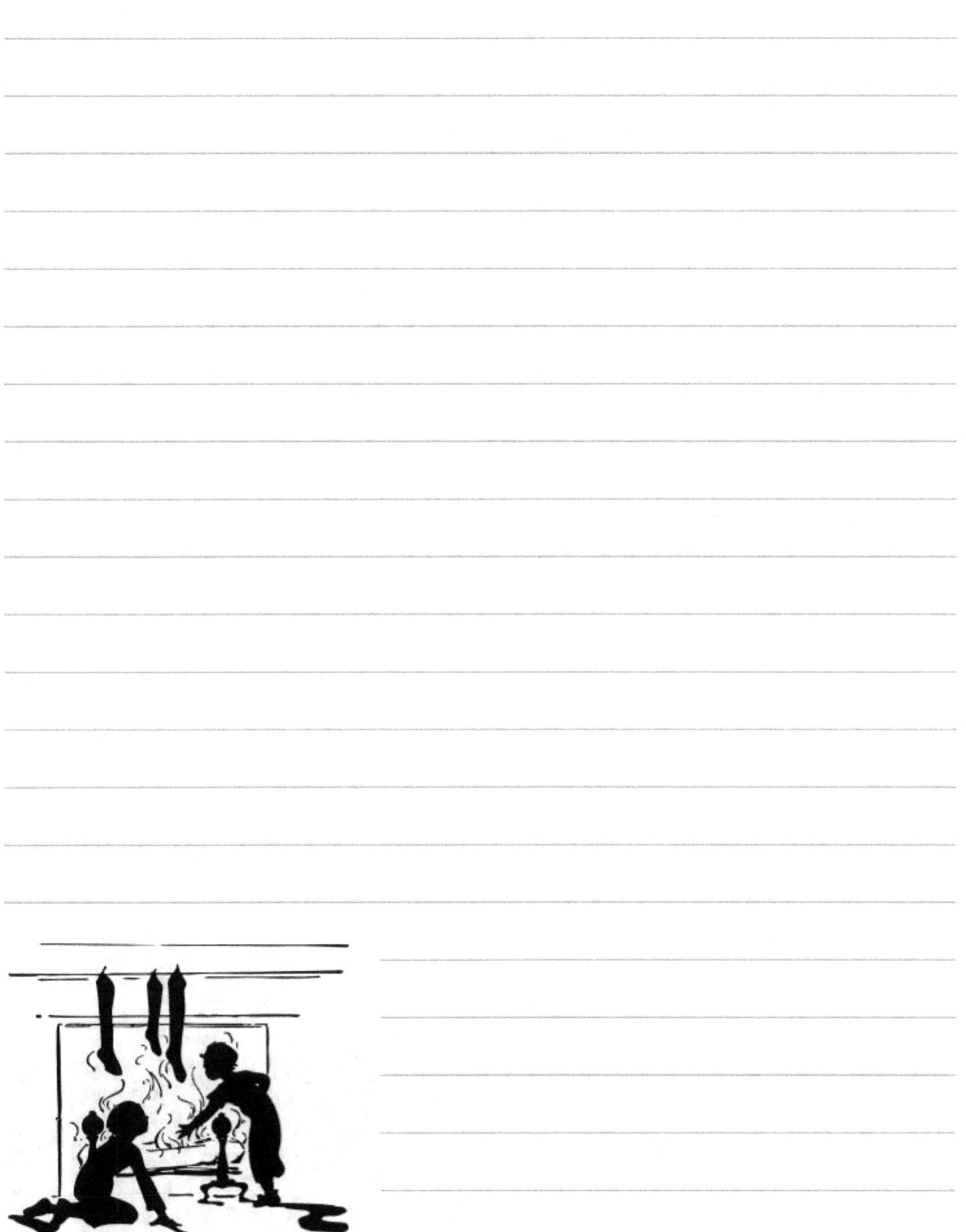

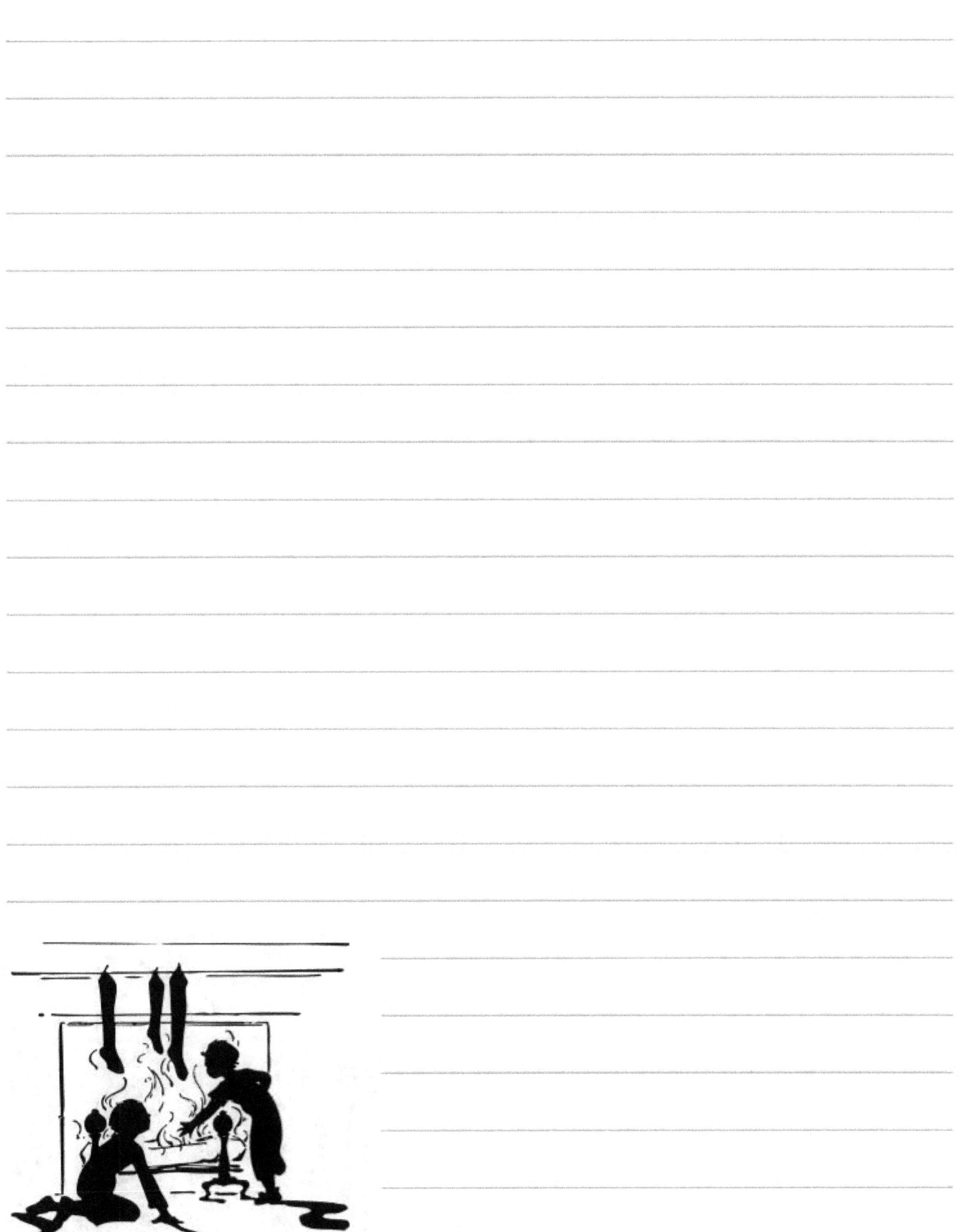

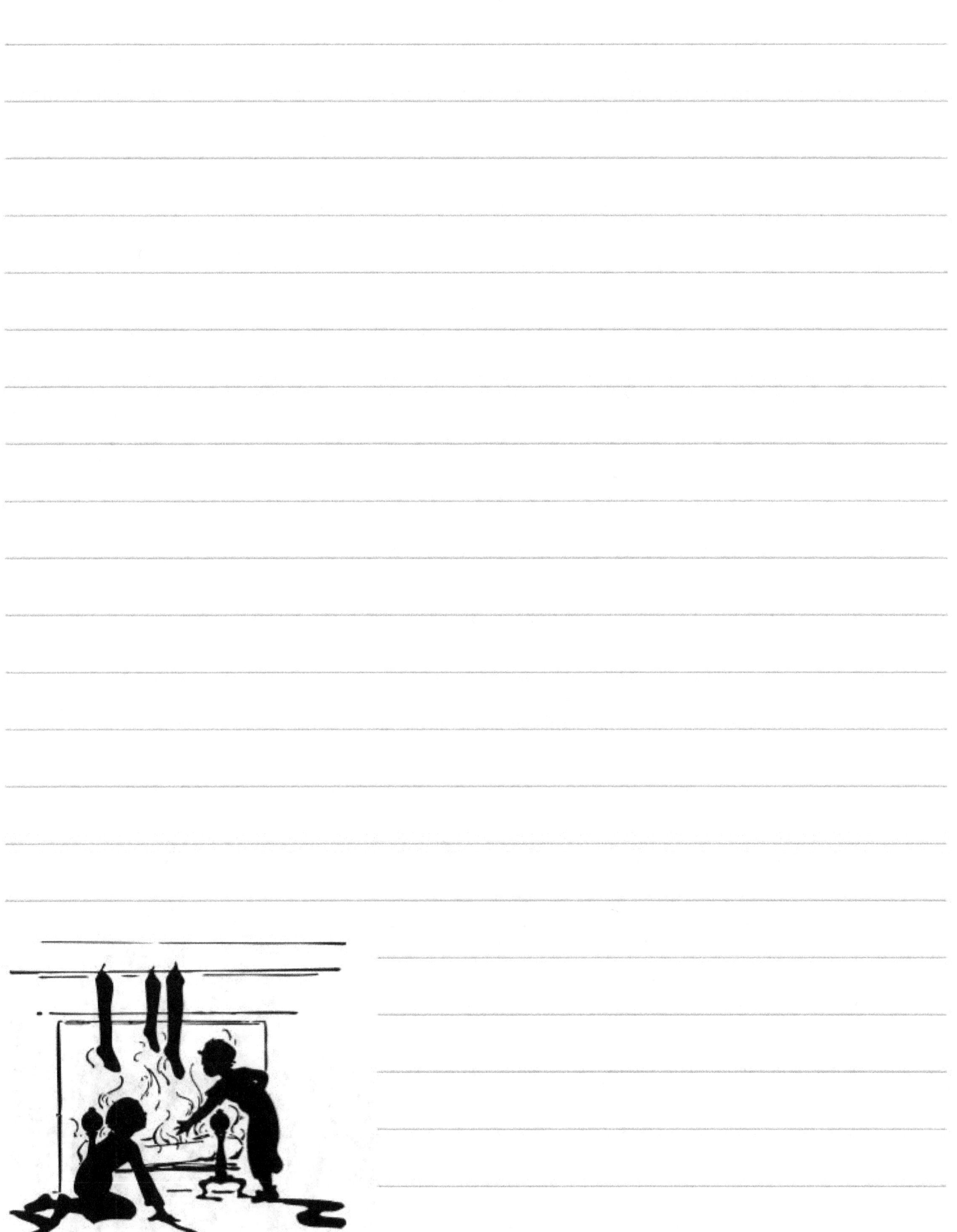

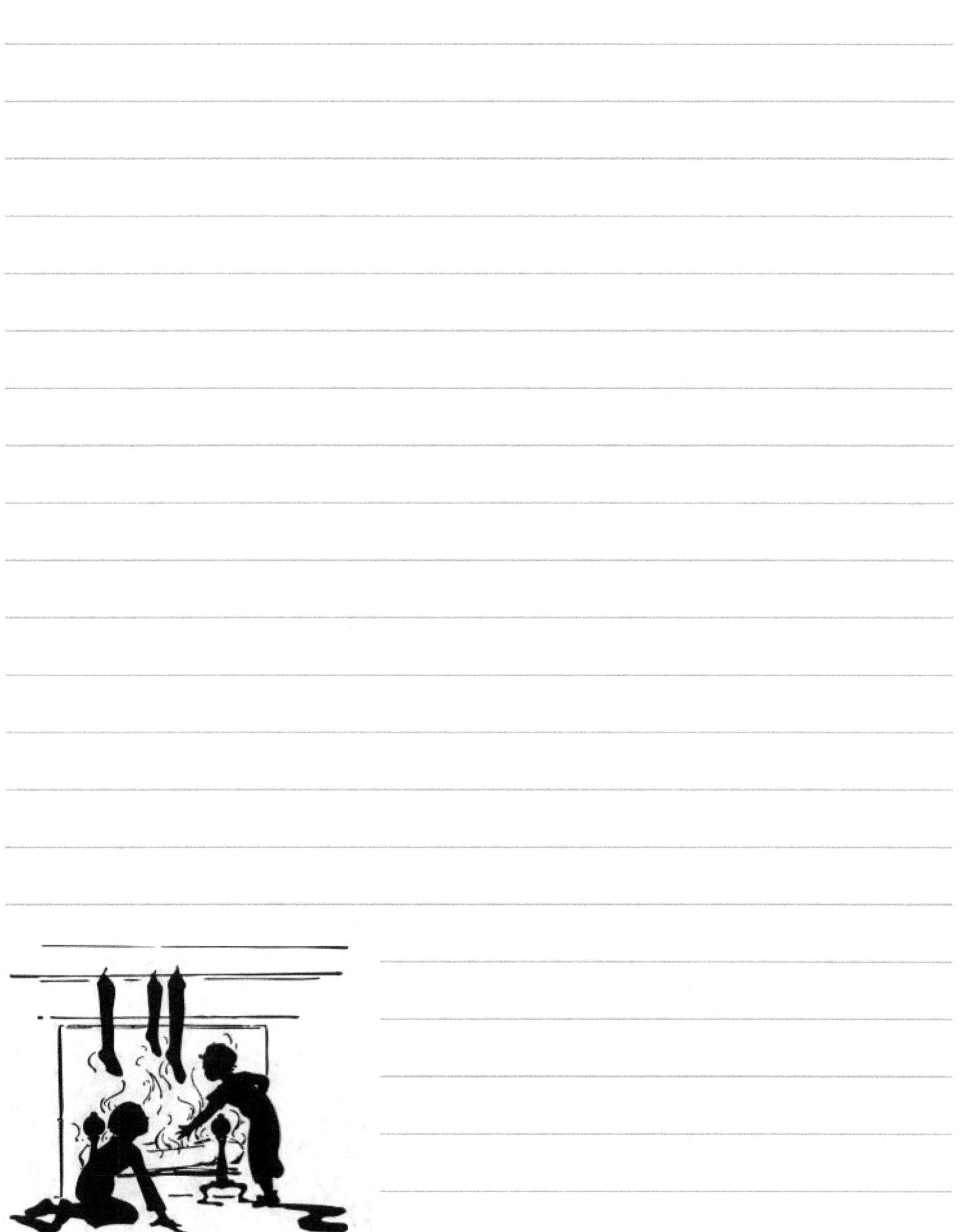

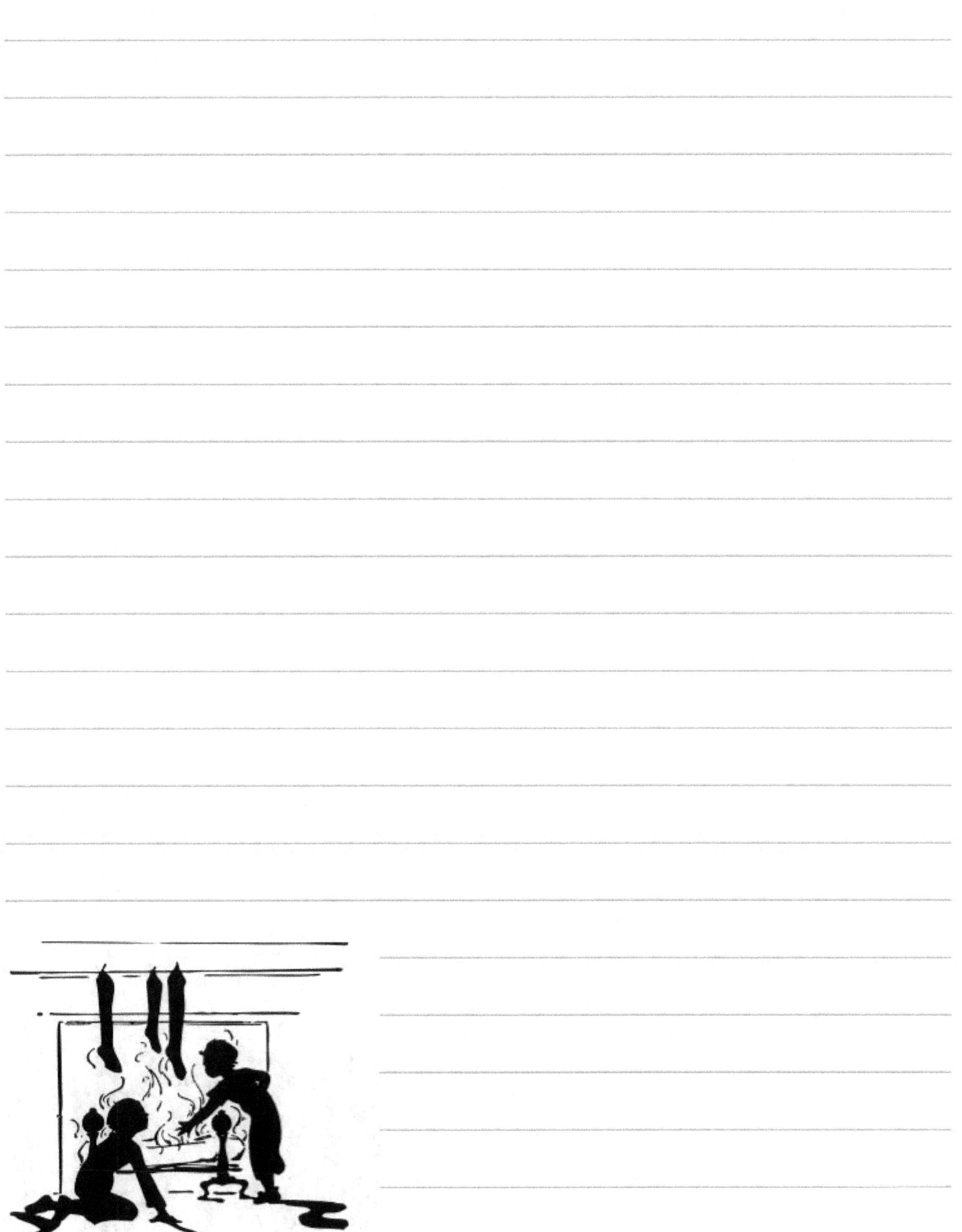

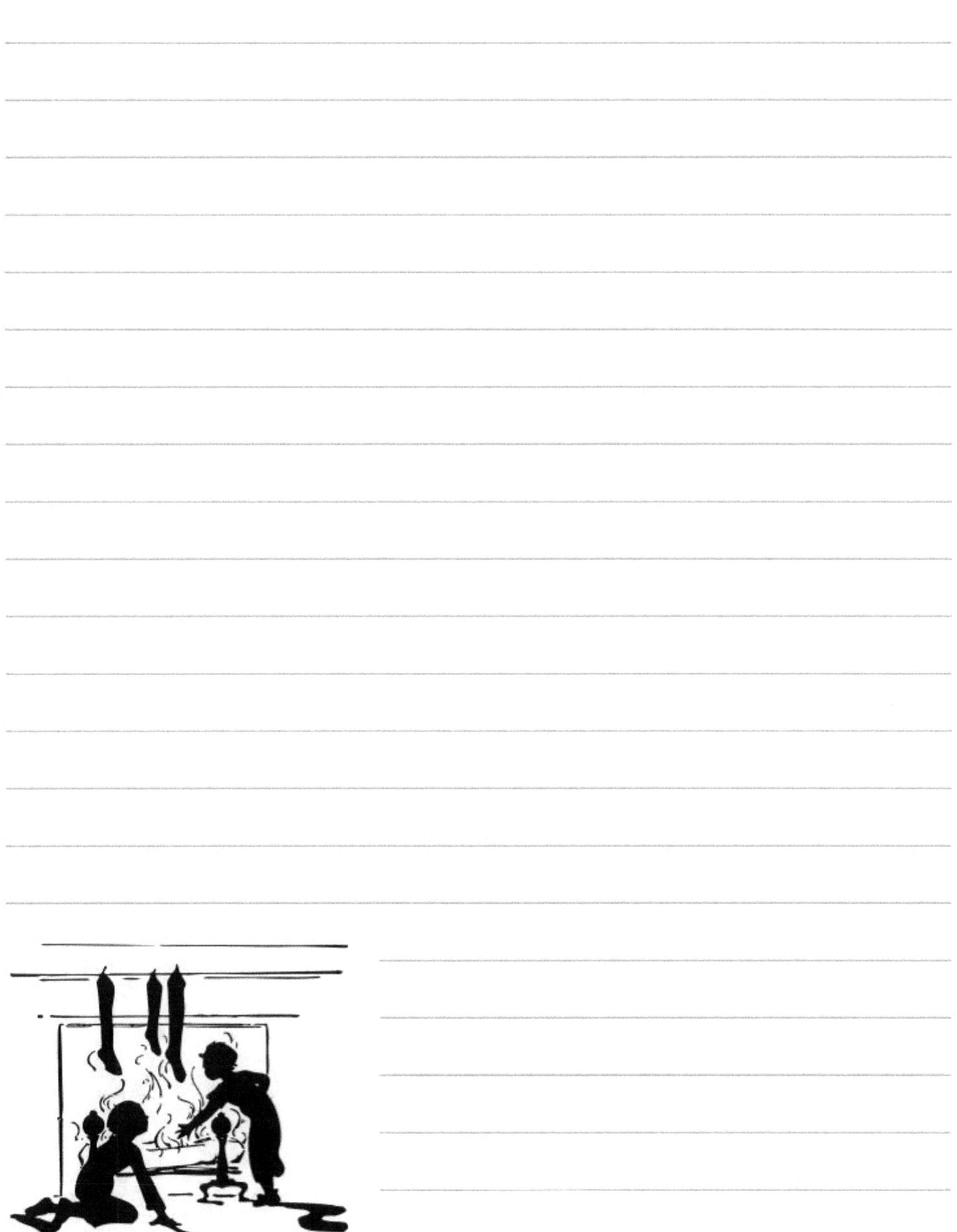